Real Estate

How to Leverage Yourself Financially and Make Money off Rental Properties by Only Paying a Fraction of the Cost

Kris Roberts

Table of Contents

Introduction

Congratulations on purchasing your personal copy of *"Real Estate: How to leverage yourself financially and make money off rental properties by only paying a fraction of the cost"*. Thank you for doing so.

The following chapters will discuss some of the many aspects of owning a rental property.

You will discover how important it is to do research before jumping into a decision that could potentially ruin you financially. You must screen your potential tenants and do background checks on each and every one of them.

The final chapter will explore the disadvantages to owning rental properties. It gives you different things to think about and explore like vacancy and some preventative measures to look out for.

There are plenty of books on this subject on the market, thanks again for choosing this one! Every effort was made to ensure it is full of as much useful information as possible. Please enjoy!

Congratulations on purchasing your personal copy of *"Real Estate: How to leverage yourself financially and make money off rental properties by only paying a fraction of the cost"*.. Thank you for doing so.

Rental Investing

It is common knowledge that investing in rental properties is one of the fastest and most secure ways to build wealth. The knowledge is not as common. The steps for buying rentals is not that different from the purchase of a house to live in. There are just a few differences. Let's take this step by step into how to invest in a rental property and start your real estate investment.

You have to do some homework before buying. You absolutely cannot skip this step. Once you have made the decision to buy a rental property, it is relatively easy to look for homes and start picking out paint colors. The first step will begin long before you ever step inside a house.

Doing homework before time will mean researching:

- You need to know what type of property you would want.
- What kind of budget do you have?
- Where do you want your investment to be located?
- What is the average rent in that area?
- How much of a return on your investment are you looking for?

Doing homework is rather difficult for one reason: You might not know the correct questions to ask. With this investment, you could get started by having a personal property. This means, that you would first live in it and when you decide to

KRIS ROBERTS

move out you could rent it out. You could just buy a rental property, and you would have a rental from the first day.

If you are a local investor, you can check on your property if there was an emergency. It will also be easier to manage the property yourself.

You must create a plan and set your criteria. When the homework is done, you can put your plan in motion. Please write down your goals and plans and look back at the many times. If you have budgeted to invest in a single family home between $100,000 to $150,000, you could get distracted by the home with a pool for $200,000. By looking back at your plans and criteria, you will be holding yourself accountable.

You will need to arrange your finances. The most common mistake is starting to search before you have your finances arranged. This has caused much heartache when they realize they can't afford the home they have found. This holds true for rental properties as well. Before you begin to shop for your rental property, you must talk to a bank to find out what you can afford. There are several different ways to get financed for real estate so make sure you look at all the options before you make a decision.

Now you can begin to look for a property. Now is the exciting part. There are several different ways to find a rental property. You can start by looking at the local MLS for available properties. There are also different websites where you can browse listings, too:

- Trulia.com

- Zillow.com

- Redfin.com

- Realtor.com

6

All of these sites will have the same listings that every real estate agent has access to. But, these do not have all the information that you might need. They also don't have all the listings, either. It is important that you get in touch with a local agent that you trust so you can get more information. The agent is paid but the seller when you buy the home so for a buyer that agent is usually free.

It is also helpful to get an agent that specializes in working with investors since they are more aware of what would make a good rental. Share the criteria you are looking for, so they will know how to help find the right property for you.

In markets like New York City, DC, or California, you can see large appreciation that any landlord would love to have. Areas like upstate New York, Wisconsin, or small town Texas would be cheaper and give you more of a cash return, nut these properties never go up in value. If you ever decide to sell, you will get the same amount that you paid for it.

When investing in a rental, you must match the demographics. A bad school district is not going to go well for a family with children just as a good school district won't set well with four single guys who want a party pad. Matching up the house, demographics, and price is important.

The main key to having a successful rental is one that will rent quickly. One that is in a good area that will attract tenants that will pay the rent on time. Here are a few characteristics that will help you narrow down where to look for properties:

- Great Schools: Schools are the key. Try to find a house around the second best elementary school area. Elementary schools are kindergarten to either fifth or sixth grade. That equals to about six years at one location. Most people will move by the time their children are out of school, but they don't like having to move before the child goes to school.

- Great Neighborhoods: Look for the worst home in the best neighborhood. Most people will be fine living in a starter home if the location is what they are looking for.

- Cheap/Small Houses: Rent values do not increase due to the size of the of the house. Small houses rent per square foot quicker than big houses will.

- Not Too Updated: You want the house to be nice, but you won't get any extra money just because you have upgraded the kitchen and bath. You want to look for nice and clean but save that money for other repairs that might, and usually do come up.

- Quiet Street: Look for houses on a cul-de-sac, with a fenced in backyard, or on a quiet street if you want to appeal to families with children and pets. If the house isn't a part of a home owner's association, look for ones with fenced in yards.

You must budget for maintenance. You have to check your numbers twice. Expenses are usually underestimated, and income is always overestimated. Base your decisions on conservative instead of liberal numbers.

As with any business venture, if it rains, it pours. You have to be prepared for all the unexpected. You many go two or three years before you have to repair something. Then all at once, you are having to spend thousands on a bathroom or possibly new central heating system.

Be prepared when things seem to be going great. The tough time will be more tolerable and not as stressful.

Another key for a successful rental is having one that creates cash from day one. To do this, you must buy a house where the mortgage and/or HOA expenses are significantly less than the rental income.

Next thing to do is to make an offer. Once you have found a property and done the walk through the next step would be to make an offer. The real estate agent will fill out all paperwork necessary, and your request will be submitted to the selling agent. The sales agent will take the offer to the seller, and the negotiations will start.

Make sure you spend only the amount that makes sense to you. Know how much cash you need and never let your emotions take over the numbers. You will always have the upper hand with negotiations if you are willing just to walk away. If a number can't be agreed upon, it will not be worth buying. Remember that it is better not to have a deal than a deal you don't like.

Price should not be the only thing to consider. It can depend on how attractive the property is and how strong the deal is. There are several other issues to keep in mind like:

- Seller's financial concessions

- Financing contingency

- Inspection contingency

- Closing date

- And much more

These are all important things you will need to discuss before you decide what to include in the offer. Talk to the real estate agent about everything that is important to the offer. When you have signed the agreement, and all the terms are agreed upon, you will have mutual acceptance.

With today's financing, you can put 20 percent down for rentals if you own less than four and then 25 percent if you own more than four.

Paying cash is good since you will be debt free. You could get a bigger property or more properties since your dollar is going further if you decide to finance them. You will also be taking advantage of today's low-interest rates.

Leverage could either be a liability or an asset. If you leverage your property, it could mean that you can buy more property with less capital. It can also be a risk.

Make sure to know when to start your due diligence. Once the price has been agreed upon, and a closing date has been set, you will start the due diligence. You will hire inspectors to perform inspections of the property and look for any problems that will cost you money in the future. If they find something, you can go back and re-negotiate as long as it is still in the timeline of the offer.

If you are trying to buy a property that is in on a hot market, it will not be wise to try to nickel-and-dime the seller. They might just decide to walk away from the deal and give it to somebody else. It is also important not to get stuck with property that has a lot of problems. Make sure you weigh your decisions very carefully and keep the goals you have in mind.

During the time between accepting and the closing, you will need to finalize the finances with the bank or lender. The company who owns the title or an attorney will take over with the facilitating of the transaction. When closing day comes, you will sign all documents and get the keys to your new property.

You should always have an exit plan. Are you keeping the house until you can retire? Are you just going to keep it until the next boom and then sell the paid capital gains and depreciation then buy in the bust? You need to know what your goal and plans are for the homes.

You can now start being a landlord. The deal is finally closed, and you are officially a landlord. If it is vacant, you can find a tenant and rent it out.

Negotiate

Always let others speak first. You may have been told sometime in your life to let the other party make the first offer. This is great advice. Do you why this will help with negotiating?

There are two reasons:

First, it will allow you to create a mid-point. Most negotiators who have some experience under their belt often find themselves just splitting the difference within the negotiations. If the other party gives their price first, the gives you the opportunity to create the mid-point in the negotiation.

Second, it is possible that the other offer is better than what you were going to make. If you needed to hire a plumber to fix a bathroom problem, you have a max budget of $600. You could tell them that you have the whole $600 to spend hoping that they don't ask for more. The plumber was only planning on charging you $400. You have already told him that you have $600, so he doesn't even need to think about any other number but the whole $600 that you have. By starting the negotiation by telling him what you have to spend, you have given them valuable information. They will use the information to get the most money out of you.

Learn to start listening and stop talking. The best thing that you can do when negotiating is just to shut up. Unfortunately, it is the hardest thing to do. People are very uncomfortable if there is a silence during the negotiating. You need these moments of silence. If you feel uncomfortable, you can bet the other person is just as nervous. The result of this awkward silence is that one party will make an offer and break that silence.

The next time you find yourself in a negotiation and the other person makes the first offer, just sit there and don't say a word. If won't matter if it is 15 seconds or 15 minutes, get them to break the silence. You will soon realize that they will interpret the silence as either disappointment or anger and will talk by revising the original offer. People who know how to negotiate use this to get inexperienced negotiators to make lower offers successively without ever having to make a counter offer.

This is probably the most useful, yet essential, negotiating strategy you can ever use.

You need to know that information is power. If I had to estimate that in about 95 percent of all negotiations that are between experienced negotiators, the one with more information will leave with the better deal. When you are negotiating, you have to be educated. You need to know everything there is to know about what you are buying as well as who you are negotiating with.

A lot of people just think that negotiation is about money, but normally it is not. Experienced negotiators know that in most cases, there is a problem to solve instead of money to discuss. Sometimes the seller might have a problem like needing to move due to a new job in just a couple of weeks that would make them take a lower offer if the buyer can close the deal so they can get moved within their time limit.

Try to get the last adjustment. If you are a good negotiator, you will be able to train the other person to do what you want them to do without them ever knowing it. Here is a way to make that happen. Make sure you ask and get the last adjustment within a negotiation. By always asking and getting the final adjustment the other people will learn to stop asking for more things when they get what they want from said negotiation.

When the other person knows that every single time they ask for anything, they always have to give something up, they will start to shy away from asking for more that they need because they will be afraid they are going to have to give something up in return.

Know that friction is your friend. Any negotiation that ends smoothly and quickly without any adjustments would appear to be a fairly good one. This might not be the case.

Make sure to keep your ego in check. Most of the time we think that the other party is looking for either better terms or more money when entering into a negotiation. Most of the time people who highly regard their negotiating skills just want their ego stroked a bit. They are not as concerned with any tangible outcome. Some are going to want every single cent they can get out of the deal. Most will give a discount just to get their ego stroked some.

Manage Your Properties

Becoming a landlord can come with many demands, but it isn't as hard as most think it is.

Sure, you are going to have a lot to do like evicting tenants who don't pay their rent, marketing your rentals, screening your tenants, making lease agreements.

Here are some tips for becoming a successful landlord:

Learn to use lease targeting. Try to schedule your lease end dates for times when the market provides the most tenant traffic. June 1st is a great move-in date.

You must treat the rental just like a business. Do you have a system in place to help with maintenance requests if you happen to be out of town? Do you set aside about ten percent of your income for necessary repairs?

Learn how to screen for bad tenants. Make sure your tenant's income is at least three times to cost of their monthly rent. Run a background and credit check, stay away from tenants that have been evicted in the past, ask for referrals from other landlords, follow Fair Housing laws.

Try your best to keep your tenants happy. It is so much cheaper to maintain a tenant than to find new ones. Fix any and all repairs as quickly as possible. Keep the property in livable conditions. Treat the residents with respect. If you can do all this, you will see less turnover and a lot more cash flow.

Make sure to get a lawyer to look at your leases. Some of the provisions that landlords put in leases are illegal. Find an attorney that is familiar with landlord-tenant laws could easily spot error within your lease and give you a court-tested document.

Reward your tenants for being good. Reward referrals, advanced rent payments, and on time payments with dinner vouchers, chocolates, or movie tickets. Basically, anything that your tenants would appreciate.

You must never discriminate. You must follow Fair Housing laws when your screen tenants. These laws make it illegal to discriminate on familial status, disability, sex, national origin, religion, color, or race.

Make sure to do move-in and out inspections. Have your tenants document any damages before they move in. Take video of the property before they move in and when the tenant moves out.

You absolutely must set hours. If you don't set some office hours, your tenants will set them for you; meaning that they will call all hours of the day and night for any and all needed repairs. Setting your hours is a perk of being a landlord.

Make sure to get professional help if you need them. Just because you have worked in construction in the past doesn't mean you should try to break up concrete to fix a problem with the plumbing. It doesn't matter if you know how to use power tools. You probably shouldn't try to fix everything.

You must document everything. There is no verbal agreement when you want to be a successful landlord. You must have signed contracts. To protect you and your tenants, you must get everything in writing.

You have to figure how much the rent needs to be. How do you know what to charge? Look in your local newspaper. Look at location. Check the internet for rent rates. Base your rent on the current market.

You must set up a Google Voice number. Never give your tenants your personal phone numbers. Set up a google voice account. This gives you a phone number that will forward to your cell number.

Set up electronic rent payments. Most tenants like to pay their bills online. It is more convenient and faster. Research different options on how to set up electronic payments.

Make sure you put in place a late policy. You need to make clear that you will charge a late fee for late rent. You must be strict with this policy. This extra income will compensate for stress created by not getting the rent on time.

Learn how to use multi-media marketing. It would be great if you could just list your property and tenants will show up. You must get your property out in front of the renters. You need to have your presence known across many marketing channels.

You must keep your family out of it. You never, ever rent to friends or family. This is a recipe for disaster. Every time you will be faced with either loss of a relationship or loss of money. Don't ever put yourself in this situation.

Make sure your lease is enforceable. Your lease needs to be air tight and sets the conditions and terms for the tenants.

Make sure you have the correct insurance. You need to have the maximum amount of property liability insurance, rental insurance, and any other insurance your state may require.

Property Management

The biggest decision you will make when you become a landlord is whether or not to hire a property management company. Most owners manage their properties by themselves or with a resident manager. There may be times when a landlord needs more help. This is where a property management company can come in handy.

These companies are a significant asset to your business, beware they are not cheap. There are some reasons why you don't want or need one. Check out the things below to see if this would be the right move for you.

What exactly does this company do? They deal with prospective tenants, which saves you worry and time. You don't have to go through the hassle of trying to market the rental properties, responding to complaints, doing maintenance or repairs, collecting rent, or pursuing evictions. A good management company will bring experience and know-how to your property. This will give you peace of mind by knowing your investment is taken care of. Last but not least, this company is an independent contractor, therefore, you don't have the issue of being an employer.

At what point should you hire a property management company? Hiring a company like this does have a lot of advantages but using them can get expensive. Dealing with these companies may not be for everyone. Think about the following facts to see if it would be feasible for you to hire a management company.

You should hire a company if:

- You have a bunch of rental units or properties.
- You live away from your properties.
- You don't want to do all the hands-on stuff.
- You don't have the time to manage.
- You have the extra money to spend on a company.
- You are overwhelmed with all the tasks you have to do.
- You don't like the thoughts of being an employer.
- Some of your properties are within the affordable housing program.

So you have decided to hire a property management company here are some things to think about:

- Find recommendations from a local apartment association or colleagues.
- Research the internet for companies.
- Interview different companies to see if they can answer the questions you have before you turn your properties over to them.

When you are a property manager, you have to cater to both a landlord and all the tenant's needs. You get caught in the middle which makes it a tough job. Some landlords manage their properties all by themselves. If you think you might want to manage your properties all by yourself, consider these things:

Professional distance and personality. The question you need to ask yourself here is, do you have a personality that will allow you to keep the relationship with tenants on a business level? If the tenant tries to break the lease, has damaged the property, or is consistently late with the rent, can you maintain your rights legally without getting emotionally involved?

Being a landlord means you have to deal with many stressful situations like demanding the rent, claiming bond money, or even evicting tenants. These are all facts of life when you are dealing with rentals. As a landlord, you must ensure you can do these things without being emotional.

Legislation and legal. When you are a landlord, you must be up to speed on all the legal issues that come up when renting properties. You should think about taking a course in property management. As landlord, you must have all the documents and agreements that will come up. You might have a dispute that involves rent payment, condition of the lease, or bond claims that might end up in a court of law. The judge will see if the landlord took the right steps and can provide the correct records to show that he followed proper protocol during the process.

If the landlord wants to evict a tenant due to failure to pay rent, they have to be able to show they provided the tenant with the right reminders, applications, and notices at the proper intervals to be able to get the court order to evict. If they can't provide all the necessary documentation, the judge won't grant the eviction, and you are stuck with a tenant who refuses to pay their rent.

The collection of rent. When being a landlord, you must be clear as to when the rent is due. Do not stop by to collect the rent. Avoid partial payments. Make sure there is at least one person that is responsible for telling you about issues with their payments.

If the tenant doesn't pay the rent on time, start by giving them written reminders of their rent. You might be able to start legal proceedings at about day ten or fourteen. Make sure you do the right steps in the right order. Keep copies of all communications but be sure not to harass the tenant. Some states have a limit on how many reminders you can give them.

How to lease the property. There might be times when your property will be vacant, and you need to find new tenants. Hopefully, someone that cares for the property and will pay the rent on time.

It all depends on the state you live in, and the tenant might have to give you somewhere between two and four weeks' notice before they can move out. If you lease your properties, there are certain steps you have to do to be able to lease it:

- Advertising is about creating competition for the property. You want to get as many people as you can to want to live there. The more applications you have; the more choices you will have to find that perfect tenant. Be sure to include your properties location and other facilities that might be near like transportation and schools. Add the features and benefits of the property and never be afraid to get detailed. Include as many pictures as you can to show the property.

- Receiving inquiries is an important part of the leasing process. You must be sure you can be reached, and you act professionally. Tenants are not going to feel comfortable renting from someone who doesn't understand what is going on and doesn't work professionally.

- Screening your tenants. You must have a thorough screening process when screening potential tenants. It is quite easy to put someone in your property but can be quite difficult to get them out of it. Have a list of questions and ask them more than once. Asking the same question by wording it differently, will allow you to see if there are any discrepancy in their answers. Talk to them both by phone and in person. Find out who they are and why they left their last residence. See if they have pets. What is their timeline for getting into the property, are they single, where do they work, and how much do they make, and references from past landlords? Call previous landlords, check your state's tenant registry to see if they have been flagged as a poor tenant.

- Accept their application. When you have done all your homework and are comfortable with your choice, approve them before someone else snatches them up. Pick a time for them to sign the lease and get the money you have decided on as far as first and last month's rent, etc.

Inspections should be done before the tenant moves in and make sure everything is good with them. After they have moved in you can do an inspection at three months and then every six months to a year. Just make sure to check with local and state laws to see what is appropriate where you live. Keep records and photographs to document anything you might find.

Rent increases and appraisals. As a landlord, you need to keep yourself up to date on what is going on in your area. Make sure you only increase rent with the terms of the lease and with what is legal where you live. You must determine what rent is going for in your area and don't increase your property's rent too high too fast. A good landlord can get thousands of dollars each year if they can understand the market.

Maintenance and repairs. The main trap that landlords find themselves in is not knowing what rights their tenants have in regards to maintenance and repairs. Especially repairs that are deemed urgent by local legislation. If there is no working toilets or hot water, the tenant has the right to get these fixed immediately. In many cases, they can have a contractor fix these and take it off the rent. As a landlord, you need to have people that you can call that will fix your repairs quickly and not charge you an arm and a leg. Having these relationships could save you a lot of money.

Time and availability. When you are a landlord, you must be sure that you are readily available and have time to deal with whatever situation might arise. It may be frustrating and costly if you have to work on holidays. Know that these can be time-consuming, especially if you don't know what you are doing. Landlords should consider having someone close they can count on to help them if they aren't available.

Record keeping, taxes, and technology. You must have the right technology. You need internet access, email, cell phone, and a financial reporting system with electronic files to keep all your records.

Costs are the main reason that people decide to be their landlord. It saves them money. These expenses are tax deductible, and you can claim them to reduce your taxable income.

Tenants

If you need to get a vacancy filled at one of your rental properties, tenants have to be able to find you. People look for properties in many places. You must advertise in many places. Here are some ways to find potential tenants:

Advertise on different websites. The internet is a good way to reach a lot of people. Craigslist.com allows you to list your property by location. Trulia.com lets you post free and can be seen all over the world. There are a lot of state sites that you could advertise on. If you want to accept government housing like Section8, Socialserve.com can help you with this market. If you have an independent website, be sure to list your property there and include your URL in your ads.

You can use social media to find tenants. Many people will use Facebook or Twitter to advertise their properties. You can put your property on Facebook's marketplace and be able to post updates, or you could send tweets to followers on Twitter.

Advertise by print media meaning use a good old fashioned newspaper. Try to get the advertisement in the weekend papers especially Sunday's since this is when papers see more traffic. You only get a few lines to get your property to stand out so make each word count. Use abbreviations when possible to save space. Putting an ad in a newspaper will cost money, but it is an excellent way to increase exposure.

Advertise on local bulletin boards. Hang flyers within the

community where your property is located. You could hang flyers on bulletin boards at bus stops, laundromats, churches, and grocery stores. Since most people walk by these bulletin boards rather quickly, you must use bold type and colors to make yours pop out at people. At the bottom of the flyers, have tear-offs that include the address, number of rooms and the contact information.

List the property with a realtor. Realtors will typically charge about one month's rent as commission maybe more. You will want to interview more than one realtor to find one that you are comfortable with. This might be an expensive way to advertise; you could save headaches and hassles when dealing with potential tenants. The property will be listed on an MLS that increases exposure.

You can find tenant through word of mouth. Never underestimate the power of spoken words. Let your current tenants know you have a vacancy. They may have relatives who are looking for a place to live. Tell everybody you know that you have a vacancy. Have flyers with you that you can hand out. You can also offer a referral fee to create an incentive.

Put for rent signs in the vacant window. You might not reach masses by putting a for rent sign it is not doing any harm either. A person passing by could be interested or know someone who is looking to rent. The phone number needs to be readable from street view.

Find tenants by offering incentives. People are drawn to discounts and deals. You might want to provide a TV or cut the rent if they can move in by a certain date. A TV that costs $300 might seem like a lot of money, but if you charge $1000 for rent and this gets someone to move in sooner, you are saving $700. The bonus is a tax write-off for the rental.

Answer all emails and phone calls and be able to show the property. Never wait to respond to phone call or email. If you don't respond promptly, some other realtor or landlord will.

Screening

If you have a house that you have tried to sell and can't, and you have decided to rent it out, trying to find good tenants who will take care of your house can be challenging but is essential. Here are some tips for choosing the right tenant:

- Use a rental application. This is a simple document that is used to collect information about the applicant and **coapplicants** so you can do background checks. The application should ask for:

    o References – never family

    o Employer contact and their job title

    o A number of pets and breed.

    o Children's ages and names

    o Income amounts and sources

    o Driver's license numbers

    o Previous addresses

    o Social Security numbers

    o Applicants' names

Depending on what laws are in your state you could charge a nonrefundable fee of $25 to $40 to cover the background checks. If they refuse to pay, you have just used a screening tool.

- Require tenants to have renter's insurance. Before the lease is signed, and during the application process, let the potential tenant know that you require proof of renter's insurance on or before the move in date. Renter's insurance covers the tenant's belongings and any damage they cause to the property. You might also consider landlord insurance to give you the coverage to protect your property.

- Meet with them in person. I shouldn't even need to say this, but you need to meet with them in the flesh and walk them through the property. Seeing them in person could give you some insight into whether they will respect your property. You will get a sense of how clean they are by seeing what they drive. Your gut feelings can go a long way. It doesn't take that much time to do a walkthrough so please don't miss this opportunity.

- You have to do background checks. The best way to find out whether they are going to be good tenants will be what their history says about them. Fees for background checks can run anywhere between $10 to $70 per adult screened. Make sure to call the applicants' employers to verify their income, too.

- You will need to wait for their check to clear. If you want to avoid any problems that could arise from accepting a personal check, ask for the deposit to be either a money order or cashier's check. If you do accept personal checks, don't take the house off the market until the check clears the bank and they have signed the lease.

- Always use a rental agreement. By having a firm contract, it will set the conditions and terms for the tenants. These should include facts such as who is allowed to live there, the date the rent is due, any penalty for late rent, etc. A great lease will spell out all policies and grounds for eviction.

- Never settle. You must be picky. Never settle out of desperation. Always have high standards. You will have low-quality tenants who might cost you a lot of money in the long run.

- Make the deposit large. You will want to make their deposit rather substantial to cover any damages just in case they turn out to be a bad apple. Never make the deposit the same amount of the monthly rent. If you are renting at $1,000, you should ask for a deposit of $1,200. If you ask for the same amount, they will likely think that it is to cover the last month's rent. You don't want that.

If you take all of this advice to heart, you will usually get a great tenant, and this makes your landlord job so much easier. Never do this halfway. The amount you could pay over the term of the lease because you chose a bad tenant is just too risky.

Non-Paying Tenants

In the most frustrating situation, hiring a lawyer can get time-consuming and expensive for both you and the tenant. These small steps can save you some grace. If you follow these steps each and every time, you will prove to be a consistent and serious landlord by following the law. There is no better way to have yourself presented.

Step 1: Keep a check on the lease documents and payment records. Yes, this sounds silly, but you need to double-check your files and make sure your tenant is late with their rent. Landlords need to keep paper records instead of trying to keep it in their heads. They might be mistaken when something was or wasn't paid. Although most states don't specify a grace period for tenants paying their rent, most leases will contain a clause that gives a three or five-day grace period. If you have double and triple checked and found that yes, they are late, then you can take whatever action that was agreed upon in the lease. A contract will state what the late fee is but if it doesn't explicitly state an amount, you can decide on what to charge. It doesn't matter how you feel about a late rent situation; it is a violation of the lease that has been signed by all parties involved. This make is a legal breach of contract.

Step 2: The Notice. The next step is to serve your tenant a late rent notice. This is a legal piece of paper that reminds them that their rent is past due. Make sure the notice includes all the fees that are owed. It should also include a warning about legal action that will follow if the rent isn't paid completely and soon. You can serve them with the paper in person, email, or tape it to their door the day after the rent is due. This will also help you in court as proof that they have a pattern of having late payments. Make sure you are keeping copies. This is not required by law, but it is recommended. It might be all a forgetful tenant needs to job their memory. The threat of legal action will make other residents take you seriously.

Step 3: Make a phone call. Calling the resident to see what is going on can be done either after or before the late rent notice has been served. Only do this one time so that you won't get hit with harassment charges. The phone call will serve the same purpose as the late rent notice. You will have an added benefit of speaking to them in person. For this reason, alone, do not substitute an email for a phone call.

Step 4: The pay or quit notice. This is more official than the late rent notice and is the first phase in the eviction process. This shows the tenant that you are serious about pursuing action and should be delivered in person on the sixth day the rent is late. It should clearly convey the intent to evict, the amount they owe you, and the date you want the money paid by. If you have an attorney, this is something they can draft up for you. Post it on their door or hand it to them personally. You could also mail them one as a back-up. You will have to wait before you can file eviction papers. This will depend on your state. It is usually about three to five day, so be sure the check with your local legislation.

Step 5: Last resort is legal action. If you have tried everything and they still haven't paid, find an eviction lawyer. At you earliest opportunity, by the end of the pay or quit period has ended, file a tenant-landlord complaint in your local court of law. In most places, it is illegal to evict someone if you haven't been through the correct court proceedings. This usually will take a few months. You have to pay a fee and complete all paperwork before you can get a hearing. When your day in court gets here, know what you are going to say and have all your documents handy.

If you are dealing with a tenant who constantly pays late or only partially pays, you have the right to inspect the property as soon as possible to ensure that the property hasn't been damaged. You can only enter with the renter's permission. When you get permission, document and take pictures of any and all damage. When you have identified what has been damaged, fix that you are obligated to and ask them to fix what is their obligation to fix. Set up another time to do another inspection to make sure they have fixed the problems. Keep everything documented just in case it goes to court.

It is not legal to lock someone out or to shut off their utilities before the process is done. Physically attempting to get the tenant out, humiliation or threats are all illegal, too. These are all questionable actions, but an ex-tenant can sue you for unlawful eviction or even harassment. Even though it is quite frustrating, just let the court do its job.

Never accept payments if you think it might go to court. In most places, receiving even a partial payment will null and void all legal actions that you have already taken. This includes pay and quits notices, and it will start the everything all over.

If there were co-signors on the lease, they are just as responsible and should be named on all the legal papers, and named in the lawsuits.

Repairs

You never want to get a phone call from a tenant that something needs to be fixed. The thought of having to replace or fix something can send panic into your life. The simple reality is that maintenance and repair is a big part of owning a rental. You may not be able to plan for a particular time for a problem to happen, you can figure out how much of your rental income you need to hold in reserve for repairs and maintenance. This gives you an idea of how much to subtract from the rent you've collected to put into a reserve account for when problems might arise.

There are a couple of ways that you can get some price estimates. If you manage your properties, make some phone calls to local contractors to get some figures. There are three common areas of repair. These will be HVAC, plumbing, and roofing. Calling a few experts in these regions and then averaging their prices will give you a decent estimate on how much a repair might cost you.

The average amount of rental income you would need to set aside each year is about one to three percent of the property's value. This revenue could be used to your advantage. You could put it in a short-term money market or other securities. If you own a $150,000 property and you can save $15,000 every year you can get a return on these funds. You might even get lucky and not have a repair for a couple of years. These savings will be substantial. What you have earned could be used to invest back into the business.

Remember that every repair that has to be done happens with an active lease. If you have to evict a tenant or if one leaves, you might have to fix the property to get it ready to put back on the market. If you can learn to be a smart landlord, you can make sure that you are never financially surprised if presented with a problem. These expenses can chip away at your profits every year. Hold onto your reserve and grow this money to help you in the long run.

You need to plan for any and all additional expenses. Changing insurance companies might require that you get a new home inspection. This can run you hundreds of dollars plus you will have the cost of the new insurance. Expenses that occur quarterly like pest inspections and prevention are separate from common repairs. By playing it safe and planning on how much income to hold back for repairs will ultimately let you enjoy a lot more of your property cash flow.

The next thing to take into consideration are the fixed expenses. These are a bit confusing since they are not fixed but occur regularly when running a rental business:

- Sewer/Water – This is usually on one bill and is usually paid by the tenant. This needs to be discussed before the lease is signed.

- Property Taxes – These are paid yearly by the landlord. You estimate them look at the next year's bill not the last. Taxes always go up every year.

- Electricity – Usually paid by tenant. Again, something to discuss before signing a lease.

- Garbage – Could be paid by either but usually tenant. Discuss before signing lease.

- Heating – Usually paid by tenant. Just another point to discuss.

- Insurance – This is usually included with the mortgage payment and is paid by landlord. Check to make sure if it is included in mortgage price, if not set aside money each month.

- Homeowners Association Fees – If the property is located in a Homeowners Association you will need to pay the fee. This is more common with upscale neighborhoods or condos. These would be paid by the tenant. Again another thing to discuss.

- Property Management Fees – If you decided to hire a company to manage your property, instead of being your own landlord, this is a fee the owner will be responsible for.

In addition to these expenses, there might be more expenses that are unique in your area. Talk to local realtors, property managers, and other landlords to see if there are any in your area. Make sure to include these.

To wrap it up, you don't want to be a failure. You want to be successful to the point of not knowing what you are going to do with your money.

Therefore, wealth created by real estate will start with the correct math.

You must understand how to calculate your expenses. You must make sure the math adds up. There is no perfect way to know what the future holds. But if you can take a simple approach and use math to help you estimate your expenses will allow you to hedge your bets the best way you can.

Profits

Numbers, you have to love numbers if you want to do well in this industry. You must love them as if they are a part of you. You must never leave numbers.

The big question is how to find the perfect property. What can I do? What to look at? How to know if it is the right one? There are different factors to consider with any potential property. The most important are the numbers. If numbers don't look right, walk away. Save yourself the time and run the numbers first to see if it works for you. If they don't add up, fine, you didn't waste your time on anything else.

So, what numbers is it that you run? What do all investors care the most about? Cash flow. Well, what exactly determines cash flow? Expenses and income. Simple as that. People act like running numbers is so complicated. It is no wonder that more people are not interested in real estate. The numbers are the easiest part of looking for a property.

Appreciation

Everyone knows the importance of return on investment. If you have rental properties, it is imperative to know how you can calculate ROI's so you can determine its effectiveness as an investment.

Since ROI calculations could be easily manipulated and variables could be excluded or included when doing a calculation figuring out the ROI might be a challenge, especially when the investor has the option of paying cash or doing a mortgage.

Return on investment is a way to measure the performance of an investment. It can also be used to compare the performance of more than one investment. To figure out ROI, the net profit is divided by the amount of money invested. The results are expressed as a percentage.

If you buy a property with cash, calculating ROI is easy. You have paid cash for a rental property for $120,000. You pay $1,000 closing cost and $9,000 for remodeling, making the total $130,000.

Now fast-forward to a year later. You collected $900 rent each month that equals to $10,800 for the entire year. For a realistic ROI deduct from that $167 each month for property taxes and insurance. That equaled $2,004 for the year. This will give you a return of $8,796.

To calculate the ROI, you will divide the return $8,796 but the investment you made at the beginning $130,000. It will look something like this: $8,796 divided by 130,000 that equals 0.067 or to break it down to a percentage 6.7 percent. Your ROI is 6.7 percent.

Let's calculate the ROI on a mortgaged property. You are purchasing the same $120,000 property as above. Instead of paying cash you have to get a mortgage. You need to put 20 percent down. That will be $24,000 for the down payment. That was calculated by taking the sales price $120,000 X 20%. The closing costs will be $3,000. There will be the same $9,000 for remodeling. This brings the total expenses to $36,000.

Some costs are associated with the mortgage. Let's say you

were able to get a 30-year loan with a fixed rate of 4%. On the borrowed $84,000, the monthly interest and principal payment on the borrowed will be $401.03. Now add $187 per month for insurance and taxes bringing your total $588.03.

Now let's look at rent. Let's say you are asking for $850 a month in rent, this will give you a cash flow of $261.97 each month. That was calculated by taking the $850 rent and subtracting the expenses of $588.03. Now fast for a year. Multiply the cash flow $261.97 by 12, and you will have your net annual income or your return on investment: 261.97 X 12 = $3,143.64.

Now, divide the cash flow ($3,143.64) by the beginning expenses which was the remodel fees, down payment, and closing costs to figure out your return on investment. So let's do the math: $3,143.64 ÷ $36,000 = 0.087. Your ROI is 8.7%.

Now, the examples above are fairly basic. They are not adding in any additional expenses that your property could generate like maintenance or repair costs these will have to be added into the calculations and will affect the ROI.

They show that your ROI will change depending on if you pay cash or finance the property. The rule is the less cash that you put into your property and the more you mortgage, the bigger your ROI is. The more cash you put into the deal and the less you finance, you will have a lesser ROI. You will have a bigger net income.

It doesn't matter what you use to figure out the ROI. The important thing to do is use the same approach with all your investment to keep accurate comparisons. If you include your equity when you evaluate one property, you will need to add it when you calculate the ROI on all your other properties, if you have more than one, to always get the right comparison.

Taxes

There isn't a landlord alive that would pay more than what they have to for operating expenses or utilities on their rentals. But millions pay more taxes than they have to. Why? Rentals provide more tax deductions than any other investment.

These benefits can make a difference with earning a profit and losing money on their properties. Here are some tax deductions that owners of small rental properties could take:

- Interest – This is a landlord's biggest expense that they can deduct. There are different interest deductions they can take, like the interest on mortgage payments, interest on credit cards they used to buy services or goods for their property.
- Depreciation – The cost of the rental property is not entirely deductible. Instead, they can get back some of the cost through depreciation. They will have to deduct a bit of the cost for several years.
- Repairs – many repairs to a rental property if they are reasonable, necessary, and ordinary are entirely deductible within the year the occurred. Examples of eligible repairs would be replacing windows, plastering, fixing leaks, repairing floors or gutters, and repainting.
- Travel – Landlords can take a tax deduction for driving they do for their rental properties. There are two options for deducting these expenses. You can deduct cost like repairs, upkeep, and gas or you can use the IRS's standard mileage rate. Check their website for the correct price. If you have to travel overnight for one of your rentals, you can deduct meals, hotel bills, airfare, or other expenses. You have to be careful here because IRS frowns on these types of deductions. If you do claim

these, please make sure to keep all records and receipts.

- Home Office – Landlords can deduct a home office expense if they meet the minimal requirement. This deduction can apply to space you use for office work plus a workshop or other space you use for your rental business.
- Independent Contractors or Employees – If you hire someone to repair your rental property, you can deduct what you paid them as a rental expense. This holds true for both a resident manager or independent contractor.
- Theft or Casualty Losses – If your property gets destroyed or damaged by flood or fire, you can get a tax deduction for either part or all of your loss. These are called casualty losses. You can't deduct the whole amount. The amount will depend on how much was destroyed and if it was covered by insurance.
- Insurance – You can deduct your insurance premiums for your rentals. This includes landlord liability, rental, flood, theft, or fire. If you have employees, you can deduct their workers' comp and health insurances.
- Professional and Legal Services – You can deduct the fees you pay to real estate investment advisors, property management companies, accountants, attorneys, or other professionals. These costs are deductible if they are paid for work that is related to your rental properties.

You might not have known that:

- People who rent to the friends and family could lose all of their tax deductions.
- A special rule permits landlords to deduct all of their rental losses each year.
- Some landlords can deduct $25,000 in property losses every year.

- You might be able to rent out a vacation home tax-free.
- If landlords carefully plan, they can deduct in one year the cost of improvements that they would have to deduct over 27 years.
- Landlords could increase the depreciation deductions they get the first years that they own their property by using segmented depreciation.

If you don't know these facts, you are paying more taxes than you should be.

Possible Disadvantages

The thought of having an easy income calls to many people. Owning rental properties like apartments, large houses, guest homes, and duplexes let the owners just sit back and collect their rent checks with nothing else to do. On paper, it looks like a lazy worker's dream job.

The so-called paychecks from rental properties are not so easy to come by. Even though rentals can generate income, you need to remember that owning a property is still a job. Before you just dive into the world of rental properties, take time to consider the cons of this arrangement so that you can make sure your strengths and weaknesses will match up with your expectations. It is a lot more complicated than just cashing the rent checks.

- Tenants can be horrible. Renters do not have a reason to care for your property. Even with the best renters, the place will be dirty when renters move out. You may need to repaint and complete basic maintenance.

  Tenants who are vindictive or just slobs might completely ransack your property knowing that the security deposit will in no way cover what they have messed up. You are going to have to spend possibly thousands of dollars to get the property back into renting conditions.

  Tenants also just stop paying rent. They know they can

do it for a while and get away with it because most landlords don't want to spend the money to take them to court. Bad tenants could set you back tens of thousands of dollars and creates numerous headaches.

- The investment will require capital. Along with the capital you need for the down payment to buy the property, you need to have liquid capital to manage it. Remember the bad tenants above, that was a lot of money to make the necessary repairs. Even if you screen for good tenants and find one, you could get hit with unexpected home repairs. As a landlord, you have to deal with problems quickly and efficiently.

  You will need a couple of hundred dollars on hand to replace a messed up water heater or thousands to repair a leaky roof. You also need landlord insurance if you are renting out your home because homeowners insurance applies only to owner-occupied properties.

- You could face possible legal consequences. Talking about legal problems, the law is on the tenant's side if you don't make needed repairs because you either don't have the money or time. The tenant has the legal right to withhold rent or even walk out on the lease if you don't take care of the property. If the lease isn't airtight, you won't have and legal rights if the tenant damages your property or doesn't pay their rent on time.

  Have a lawyer that is experienced in rental real estate to look at your lease. Check your insurance policies to make sure you have adequate coverage. If you don't have proper coverage, your tenant can take you to court if they or guests of theirs are injured on your property.

- You will be faced with time-consuming efforts. Unexpected repairs will take time to figure out. The whole process of ownership and management will take time.

You need to account for energy and time that is required to find suitable tenants with applications, credit reports, and interviews. You have to keep on top of the resident's needs, inquiries, rent checks, and deposits. The tenant is paying you for a place to stay and the property. This all takes time and know-how.

Your income is not going to pour in without many hours that you have set aside for managing the property. This can be a problem if you are working a 9 – 5 job while renting out properties. You could hire a property management firm but this is going to cost you money, and that reduces your income amount. It would be a good idea to talk with some property management companies to find out what services they offer and how much they charge.

- Your bottom line could bite back. There is a risk involved when owning a rental property. The market might not behave like you want it to like when your property depreciates instead of appreciates. Problems could befall the property like bad tenants or extremely expensive repairs. You could have problems filling your vacancies. You could guard against the setbacks by diversifying your portfolios or properties. This way your financial future is not tied up to one rental property.

The government will come wanting its fair share of your money. You must document your expenses and income, so the government doesn't take more than what is due to them. If you ever have any questions about your property, talk with an accountant to stay away from any surprises.

- How to convert a residence to a part-time rental. You need to be careful about the small print with your rental property ambitions. They could haunt you. Tax laws will not allow you to exit the premises for a few weeks every year so you can get a bit more income and use it as a write-off. You can rent out your home for the extra money, but you can't take any more deductions.

  Any property you own is thought of as a primary residence if you occupy the home more than 14 days of over ten percent of the time renters occupy it, whichever scenario is greater. If it is still considered a primary residence, even after you have converted it into a rental, you can't deduct any expenses when it comes tax time. Since it is still a primary residence, you can deduct the mortgage interest. If you want to benefit from the deductions, you will need to talk to an accountant before you start converting it into a rental, so you won't be disappointed at tax time.

If owning rentals properties sound appealing to you and in-depth management is beyond your skills, scheduling limits, or interests, think about hiring a property management company. For the ideal scenario, you could make income from rent, but someone will be in charge of the upkeep, rent collecting, and finding new tenants. You will need to interview more than one manager to figure out which company will work best for you.

Vacancies

Most landlords may have to deal with a vacancy from time to time. You will have a vacancy when you put your property on the market for the first time when you have to evict a tenant, when a tenant breaks their lease, or when a lease expires. There will be bills you will still have to pay when your property is vacant. You must be financially prepared. Here are some costs you might have to deal with when your property is vacant.

Mortgage – If you don't own your rental property, you are still responsible for paying the mortgage. The rent usually helps to offset this payment.

Taxes – You are still responsible for paying property taxes on your properties whether or not it has a tenant.

Utilities – If the utilities are in your name, you are the responsible party for paying these. The bill will probably be very low since no one is living there. If you think it might be a long-term vacancy, you could have these cut off to save some money. The main drawback here would be if temps in the area were to drop below freezing, the water pipes might burst if there is no heat in the unit.

Insurance – You will still have to pay insurance on the property. This might include liability, flood, and hazard insurance.

There are a few more costs that you might have to deal with if you have to evict tenants or if the tenant owes you money for damage to the property.

Eviction costs – You need to factor the cost of eviction. There are court costs, and the cost to have a sheriff lock them out of the property. This cost will grow if you decide to hire an attorney to help you with the eviction proceedings. You may also lose money due to damages the tenant did to the property or other breaches of contract.

Security deposit – If you collected a security deposit from the tenant, you might be able to offset some costs with this money. You would normally have to return this to the tenant at the end of their lease. If the tenant broke the lease, stopped paying their rent, or breached the lease in other ways, you might be able to keep some of the deposit to cover the costs. The amount you can get from a tenant varies by state but is usually no more than two month's rent.

If the amount of deposit isn't enough to cover all the money the tenant owes you, you can try to sue them in small claims court. Even if you are awarded the money, it is still tough to collect.

Preventative Measures

If you still want to tap into your inner Baron, here are some smart moves to help you get started.

Recognize that this will be a business. Being a landlord is very different that being a homeowner. It is a business, and you must treat as such. Most people won't have a good business plan. This is not a hands-off investment. It is not a passive stream of revenue. You have to be involved. It will require your time and skills.

If you borrow money, you will need to have about 20 percent for the down payment. If it is your first property, your income will have to be enough to handle both mortgages.

You will need to start small. Start with a single home or a small multiple-unit. You might think about getting a partner to see if this is something you want to do. Single-family properties are the easiest to buy when looking for investment properties. Condos require a bigger down payment and monthly fees. If you can start with a single house, this will allow you to get a feel for bookkeeping, maintenance, and other work it requires. Try to find a property without high maintenance features like elaborate landscaping.

Never invest in someplace you don't know. Finding a good location is true when finding a rental property. A home that's a steal could be priced due to a bad neighborhood that no one wants to live in like bad schools or high crime rates. Investing in out of state is a gamble also. Buy within neighborhoods that you know or have researched thoroughly is the smart way to go.

You have to figure out the correct rent. Rent differs everywhere in the United States. Local realtors can give you an average of what the rent would be in the area you are looking at. You will have to figure out if that will cover your costs. People look at the loan and think they can cover that, and everything is fine. You will need to pay for insurance and taxes. Remember to budget for maintenance as we have stated before.

Don't be afraid to get your hands dirty. When you start with a single home, you will find that if you can manage it by yourself, you will save some money. This is where your special skill come in handy. The better you can handle tools, the easier it will be to maintain your property. You won't have to hire expensive electricians and plumbers each time something breaks. If you have put off fixing thing in your own house, then renting out other properties will not be the business for you.

If you need professional help, get it. When you decide on a property, you will want to talk with a real estate lawyer to draft you a good lease and learn what rights you and the tenant has. You might want to hire an accountant or possibly have some general contractors, electricians, and plumbers on call. As we have talked about before there is also the option of paying for a property management company.

Above all else keep your tenants happy. The most costs that come with being a landlord is vacancy. Every time someone moves out you will be spending money and sometimes a lot of it. This means you must find and keep good tenants. Remember to run those background checks on all prospective tenants to find the right renters. Happy tenants are very important. They are your customers. The way to keep them happy is keeping the property in good working order and treating them with respect. If you can do that, you will be building wealth that you will feel great about.

Conclusion

Thank for making it through to the end of *"Real Estate: How to leverage yourself financially and make money off rental properties by only paying a fraction of the cost"*. Let's hope it was informative and able to provide you with all of the tools you need to achieve your goals.

The next step is to get your finances in order and start your research. Don't forget to do all the steps listed in this book. Yes, it can be overwhelming but take it one step at a time, and you will find success soon.

Finally, if you found this book useful in any way, a review on Amazon is always appreciated!

www.ingramcontent.com/pod-product-compliance
Lightning Source LLC
Chambersburg PA
CBHW071828170526
45167CB00003B/1458

* 9 7 8 1 5 4 4 0 3 7 3 4 9 *